LITTLE WOMEN

Louisa May Alcott

Spark Publishing
A Division of Barnes & Noble
120 Fifth Avenue
New York, NY 10011
www.sparknotes.com

ISBN-13: 978-1-5866-3477-3
ISBN-10: 1-5866-3477-1

Please submit changes or report errors to www.sparknotes.com/errors.

Printed and bound in The United States.

7   9   10   8   6

INTRODUCTION: STOPPING TO BUY SPARKNOTES ON A SNOWY EVENING

Whose words these are you *think* you know.
Your paper's due tomorrow, though;
We're glad to see you stopping here
To get some help before you go.

Lost your course? You'll find it here.
Face tests and essays without fear.
Between the words, good grades at stake:
Get great results throughout the year.

Once school bells caused your heart to quake
As teachers circled each mistake.
Use SparkNotes and no longer weep,
Ace every single test you take.

Yes, books are lovely, dark, and deep,
But only what you grasp you keep,
With hours to go before you sleep,
With hours to go before you sleep.

CONTENTS

NOTE: This SparkNote uses the 2000 Modern
Library edition of *Little Women*. Chapters 1–23
are grouped together as Part One, and Chapters
24–27 are grouped together as Part Two.

CONTEXT

LOUISA MAY ALCOTT WAS BORN on November 29, 1832, the second daughter of Amos Bronson and Abigail "Abba" May Alcott. She was raised in Concord, Massachusetts, a small town to the north of Boston that was home to many great writers of the day. Ralph Waldo Emerson, Nathaniel Hawthorne, and Henry David Thoreau were neighbors to the Alcotts. All of these writers were part of the transcendentalist movement during the New England Renaissance. Transcendentalists believed that one could find spirituality through nature and reason. They were an optimistic group who believed humans were capable of great thoughts, and they advocated nonconformity and being true to one's inner self.

Amos Bronson Alcott was not a particularly responsible father or husband, although he was an enthusiastic transcendentalist philosopher, abolitionist, and teacher. He failed to provide enough money to support his family, and their poverty was so dire that in twenty years, they moved twenty times. Louisa's mother acted as head of the household, and when Louisa grew older, she also took on much of the burden.

Louisa May Alcott had an older sister, Anna, and two younger sisters, Lizzie and Abba May. These names are noticeably similar to the names Alcott gives her characters in *Little Women* (Meg, Beth, and Amy). Her sister Lizzie died at age twenty-two after a bout of scarlet fever. Alcott also had a brother, Dapper, who died in infancy.

Alcott was educated at home by her father. She loved to read and write and enjoyed borrowing books from Emerson's large library. As a child, Alcott struggled with the ladylike behavior that was expected of girls in the nineteenth century. Though she was required to be calm and stay at home, Alcott was a tomboy whose favorite childhood activity was running wild through the fields of Concord. She had an unladylike temper that she struggled to control.

Like Jo March in *Little Women*, Alcott could not get over her disappointment in not being a boy, since opportunities for women were limited. When the Civil War broke out in 1861, Alcott had an urge to go and fight in it. Like most transcendentalists, she supported the Northern side of the conflict because she was against slavery. But since she was female and thus could not join the military, she signed up to be a Union nurse and was stationed in Washington, D.C. Later in life, Alcott became active in the women's suffrage movement in the United States, whose supporters sought to extend the right to vote to women. Alcott's feminist sympathies are expressed through the character of Jo March in *Little Women*.

Though she never married or had a family of her own, Alcott was devoted to her parents and her sisters. She understood that for women, having a family meant professional loss, and having a profession meant personal loss. *Little Women* dramatizes this struggle between the desire to help one's family and the desire to help oneself.

Alcott caught pneumonia while working as a nurse in the Civil War. She was treated with calomel, a mercury compound, and this treatment gave her mercury poisoning. For twenty years Alcott was weak, suffered intense pain, and was plagued by hallucinations that could only be controlled with opium. Her right hand hurt her so badly that she had to learn how to write with her left hand. She also lost her hair because of the illness. Alcott died on March 6, 1888, and was buried in Sleepy Hollow Cemetery in Concord, Massachusetts, alongside her father, Emerson, Hawthorne, and Thoreau.

Alcott is most famous for her domestic tales for children, which brought her fame and fortune during her lifetime. Alcott also wrote sensationalist gothic novels, such as *A Long Fatal Love Chase*, and serious adult novels, such as *Moods* and *Work*, which received middling reviews. *Little Women* and Alcott's other domestic novels have enjoyed more popularity than her novels of other genres. Alcott did not particularly like *Little Women*; she wrote it at the request of her publisher, and upon its great success, worried that she was doing nothing more than writing "moral pap" fit for children.

Little Women possesses many qualities of the didactic genre, a class of works that have a moral lesson. *Little Women* does not preach directly to the reader, however, as did much didactic fiction of its time. The narrator refrains from too much explicit moralizing, allowing us to draw our own lessons from the outcome of the story.

Because Jo learns to behave and becomes a lady at the end of the novel, it is possible to assume that Alcott wants to teach her readers that conformity is good. Interestingly, however, *Little Women* has been championed by feminists for more than a century because untamed Jo is so compellingly portrayed. Also, in the novel's characterization of the March sisters, rebellion is often valued over conformity. So while *Little Women* can be called a didactic novel, the question of what it teaches remains open.

PLOT OVERVIEW

Alcott prefaces *Little Women* with an excerpt from John Bunyan's seventeenth-century work *The Pilgrim's Progress*, an allegorical novel about leading a Christian life. Alcott's story begins with the four March girls—Meg, Jo, Beth, and Amy—sitting in their living room, lamenting their poverty. The girls decide that they will each buy themselves a present in order to brighten their Christmas. Soon, however, they change their minds and decide that instead of buying presents for themselves, they will buy presents for their mother, Marmee. Marmee comes home with a letter from Mr. March, the girls' father, who is serving as a Union chaplain in the Civil War. The letter inspires the girls to bear their burdens more cheerfully and not to complain about their poverty.

On Christmas morning, the girls wake up to find books, probably copies of *The Pilgrim's Progress,* under their pillows. Later that day, Marmee encourages them to give away their breakfast to a poor family, the Hummels. Their elderly neighbor, Mr. Laurence, whom the girls have never met, rewards their charitable activities by sending over a feast. Soon, Meg and Jo are invited to attend a New Year's Party at the home of Meg's wealthy friend, Sally Gardiner. At the party, Jo retreats to an alcove, and there meets Laurie, the boy who lives with Mr. Laurence. While dancing, Meg sprains her ankle. Laurie escorts the sisters home. The Marches regret having to return to their daily routine after the holiday festivities.

Jo visits Laurie when he is sick, and meets his grandfather, Mr. Laurence. She inadvertently insults a painting of Mr. Laurence in front of the man himself. Luckily, Laurie's grandfather admires Jo's spunk, and they become friends. Soon, Mr. Laurence meets all the sisters, and Beth becomes his special favorite. Mr. Laurence gives her his deceased granddaughter's piano.

The girls have various adventures. Amy is caught trading limes at school, and the teacher hits her as punishment. As a result, Mrs. March withdraws her daughter from school. Jo refuses to let Amy go with her to the theater. In retaliation, Amy burns Jo's manuscript, and Jo, in her anger, nearly lets Amy drown while ice-skating. Pretty Meg attends her friend Annie Moffat's party and, after allowing the other girls to dress her up in high style, learns that appearances are not everything. While at the party, she hears that people think she intends to marry Laurie for his money.

That year, the Marches form the Pickwick Club, in which they write a family newspaper. In the spring, Jo smuggles Laurie into one of the club meetings, and he becomes a member, presenting his new circle with a postbox. At the beginning of June, the Marches decide to neglect their housework. At the end of a lazy week, Marmee takes a day off too. The girls spoil a dinner, but everyone ends up laughing over it. One day, Laurie has English friends over, and the Marches go on a picnic with them. Later, Jo gets a story published for the first time.

One dark day, the family receives a telegram saying that Mr. March is sick in the hospital in Washington, D.C. Marmee goes to tend to him, and Jo sells her hair to help finance the trip. Chaos ensues in Marmee's wake, for the girls neglect their chores again. Only Beth goes to visit the Hummels, and after one of her visits, she contracts scarlet fever from the Hummel baby. Beth teeters on the brink of death until Marmee returns. Meanwhile, Amy spends time at Aunt March's house in order to escape the disease. Beth recovers, though not completely, and Mr. Brooke, Laurie's tutor, falls in love with Meg, much to Jo's dismay. Mr. Brooke and Meg are engaged by the end of Part One.

Three years pass before Part Two begins. Mr. March is home from the war, and Laurie is nearly done with school. Soon, Meg marries and moves into a new home with Mr. Brooke. One day, Amy decides to have a lunch for her art school classmates, but poor weather ruins the festivities. Jo gets a novel published, but she must cut it down in order to please her publishers. Meanwhile, Meg struggles with the duties of keeping house, and she soon gives birth to twins, Demi and Daisy. Amy gets to go to Paris instead of Jo, who counted on the trip, because their Aunt Carroll prefers Amy's lady-like behavior in a companion.

Jo begins to think that Beth loves Laurie. In order to escape Laurie's affections for her, Jo moves to New York so as to give Beth a chance to win his affections. There Jo meets Professor Bhaer, a poor German language instructor. Professor Bhaer discourages Jo from writing sensationalist stories, and she takes his advice and finds a simpler writing style. When Jo returns home, Laurie proposes to her, but she turns him down. Beth soon dies.

Amy and Laurie reunite in France, and they fall in love. They marry and return home. Jo begins to hope that Professor Bhaer will come for her. He does, and they marry a year later. Amy and Laurie have a daughter named Beth, who is sickly. Jo inherits Plumfield, Aunt March's house, and decides to turn it into a boarding school for boys. The novel ends with the family happily gathered together, each sister thankful for her blessings and for each other.

PLOT OVERVIEW

CHARACTER LIST

Josephine March The protagonist of the novel, and the second-oldest March sister. Jo, who wants to be a writer, is based on Louisa May Alcott herself, which makes the story semi-autobiographical. Jo has a temper and a quick tongue, although she works hard to control both. She is a tomboy, and reacts with impatience to the many limitations placed on women and girls. She hates romance in her real life, and wants nothing more than to hold her family together.

Meg March The oldest March sister. Responsible and kind, Meg mothers her younger sisters. She has a small weakness for luxury and leisure, but the greater part of her is gentle, loving, and morally vigorous.

Beth March The third March daughter. Beth is very quiet and very virtuous, and she does nothing but try to please others. She adores music and plays the piano very well.

Amy March The youngest March girl. Amy is an artist who adores visual beauty and has a weakness for pretty possessions. She is given to pouting, fits of temper, and vanity; but she does attempt to improve herself.

Laurie Laurence The rich boy who lives next door to the Marches. Laurie, whose real name is Theodore Laurence, becomes like a son and brother to the Marches. He is charming, clever, and has a good heart.

Marmee The March girls' mother. Marmee is the moral role model for her girls. She counsels them through all of their problems and works hard but happily while her husband is at war.

Mr. March The March girls' father and Marmee's husband. He serves in the Union army as a chaplain. When he returns home, he continues acting as a minister to a nearby parish.

Mr. Brooke Laurie's tutor. Mr. Brooke is poor but virtuous.

Frederick Bhaer A respected professor in Germany who becomes an impoverished language instructor in America. Mr. Bhaer lives in New York, where he meets Jo. He is kind and fatherly.

Mr. Laurence Laurie's grandfather and the Marches' next-door neighbor. Mr. Laurence seems gruff, but he is loving and kind.

Hannah The Marches' loyal servant.

Aunt March A rich widow and one of the March girls' aunts. Although crotchety and difficult, Aunt March loves her nieces and wants the best for them.

Daisy Meg and Mr. Brooke's daughter. Daisy is the twin of Demi. Her real name is Margaret.

Demi Meg and Mr. Brooke's son and Daisy's twin. Demi's real name is John Laurence.

Mrs. Kirke The woman who runs the New York boarding house where Jo lives.

Kate Vaughn One of Laurie's British friends. At first, Kate turns up her nose at the bluntness and poverty of the Marches. She later decides that she likes them, however, showing that she is able to overcome her initial prejudice.

Sallie Gardiner Meg's rich friend. Sallie represents the good life to Meg, and Meg often covets Sallie's possessions.

Aunt Carrol One of the March girls' aunts. Aunt Carrol is ladylike, and she takes Amy with her to Europe.

Florence Aunt Carrol's daughter. Florence accompanies her aunt and Amy to Europe.

Fred Vaughn One of the Vaughn siblings. Fred is Laurie's friend, but he soon develops a romantic interest in Amy.

Esther Aunt March's servant. Esther is a French Catholic.

Annie Moffat Another wealthy friend of Meg's. Annie is fashionable and social, and she wears stylish clothing that Meg envies.

Ned Moffat The older brother of Meg's friend Annie Moffat.

Frank Vaughn One of the Vaughn siblings. Frank is sickly.

Grace Vaughn The youngest sister of the Vaughn family. Grace and Amy become friends on a picnic.

Dr. Bangs A doctor who tends to Beth when she is ailing.

The Hummels A family that lives near the Marches. The Hummels are poor and in bad health.

ANALYSIS OF MAJOR CHARACTERS

JO MARCH

The main character of *Little Women,* Jo is an outspoken tomboy
with a passion for writing. Her character is based in large part on
Louisa May Alcott herself. Jo refuses Laurie's offer of marriage,
despite the fact that everyone assumes they will end up together. In
the end, Jo gives up her writing and marries Professor Bhaer, which
can be seen either as a domestic triumph or as a professional loss,
since Jo loses her headstrong independence.

Because she displays good and bad traits in equal measure, Jo is
a very unusual character for nineteenth-century didactic fiction. Jo's
bad traits—her rebelliousness, anger, and outspoken ways—do not
make her unappealing; rather, they suggest her humanity. Jo is a
likely precursor to a whole slew of lovably flawed heroes and heroines of children's books, among them Mark Twain's Tom Sawyer.

BETH MARCH

The third March sister, Beth is very shy and quiet. Like Meg, she
always tries to please other people, and like Jo, she is concerned
with keeping the family together. Beth struggles with minor faults,
such as her resentment for the housework she must do.

Beth resembles an old-fashioned heroine like those in the novels
of the nineteenth-century English author Charles Dickens. Beth is a
good person, but she is also a shade too angelic to survive in Alcott's
more realistic fictional world. With Beth's death, Alcott lets an old
type of heroine die off. The three surviving March sisters are strong
enough to live in the changing real world.

Beth is close to Jo; outgoing Jo and quiet Beth both have antiso-
cial tendencies. Neither of them wants to live in the world the way it
is, with women forced to conform to social conventions of female
behavior. Similarly, it is not surprising that Meg and Amy are particularly close to each other, since generous Meg and selfish Amy
both find their places within a gendered world.

AMY MARCH

The youngest March sister, Amy is an artistic beauty who is good at manipulating other people. Unlike Jo, Amy acts as a perfect lady because it pleases her and those around her. She gets what she wants in the end: popularity, the trip to Europe, and Laurie. Amy serves as a foil—a character whose attitudes or emotions contrast with, and thereby accentuate, those of another character—for Jo, who refuses to submit to the conventions of ladyhood. Both artists struggle to balance society's expectations with their own natural inclinations. The more genuine of the two and the more generous, Jo compares favorably to Amy. Both characters, however, are more lovable and real for their flaws.

MEG MARCH

The oldest March sister, Meg battles her girlish weakness for luxury and money, and ends up marrying a poor man she loves. Meg represents the conventional and good; she is similar to her mother, for whom she was named. Meg sometimes tries to alter who she is in order to please other people, a trait that comes forth when she allows other girls to dress her up like a rich girl at her friend Annie Moffat's house. She becomes an agreeable housewife, pretending to like politics because her husband does, and forgoing luxury because her husband is poor.

LAURIE LAURENCE

The Marches' charming, fun, and intelligent next-door neighbor, Laurie becomes particularly close to Jo but ends up marrying Amy. In between the publication of Part One and Part Two, Alcott received many letters asking her to marry Jo to Laurie. Perhaps to simultaneously please her readers and teach them a lesson, Alcott had Jo get married, but not to Laurie.

Laurie struggles with his grandfather's expectations of him, in a similar manner to the way Jo struggles with becoming a lady. Laurie is not manly enough for his grandfather because he does not want to enter the business world. Likewise, Jo is not feminine enough for her sisters because she swears, soils her gloves, and speaks her mind at all times.

THEMES, MOTIFS & SYMBOLS

THEMES

Themes are the fundamental and often universal ideas explored in a literary work.

WOMEN'S STRUGGLE BETWEEN
FAMILIAL DUTY AND PERSONAL GROWTH

While on the surface a simple story about the four March girls' journeys from childhood to adulthood, *Little Women* centers on the conflict between two emphases in a young woman's life—that which she places on herself, and that which she places on her family. In the novel, an emphasis on domestic duties and family detracts from various women's abilities to attend to their own personal growth. For Jo and, in some cases, Amy, the problem of being both a professional artist and a dutiful woman creates conflict and pushes the boundaries set by nineteenth-century American society.

At the time when Alcott composed the novel, women's status in society was slowly increasing. As with any change in social norms, however, progress toward gender equality was made slowly. Through the four different sisters, Alcott explores four possible ways to deal with being a woman bound by the constraints of nineteenth-century social expectations: marry young and create a new family, as Meg does; be subservient and dutiful to one's parents and immediate family, as Beth is; focus on one's art, pleasure, and person, as Amy does at first; or struggle to live both a dutiful family life and a meaningful professional life, as Jo does. While Meg and Beth conform to society's expectations of the role that women should play, Amy and Jo initially attempt to break free from these constraints and nurture their individuality. Eventually, however, both Amy and Jo marry and settle into a more customary life. While Alcott does not suggest that one model of womanhood is more desirable than the other, she does recognize that one is more realistic than the other.

THE DANGER OF GENDER STEREOTYPING

Little Women questions the validity of gender stereotypes, both male and female. Jo, at times, does not want to be a conventional female. In her desires and her actions, she frustrates typical gender expectations. She wants to earn a living, for example—a duty conventionally reserved for men. Also, she wears a dress with a burn mark to a party, evidence that she does not possess tremendous social grace, a quality that nineteenth-century American society cultivated in women. Similarly, there are times when Laurie does not want to be a conventional man. He wants to pursue music, at that time a culturally feminine pursuit, instead of business, a culturally masculine pursuit. Even his nickname, Laurie, which he uses in favor of his much more masculine given name, Theodore, suggests his feminine side. Alcott bestows the highest esteem upon Jo and Laurie, who, in their refusal to embody gender stereotypes, willingly expose themselves to particular obstacles.

THE NECESSITY OF WORK

Over the course of *Little Women,* the March sisters try to find happiness through daily activities, their dreams, and each other; but when they do not engage in any productive work, they end up guilty and remorseful. When they indulge in selfishness by dressing up in finery, hoarding limes, neglecting chores, or getting revenge, the girls end up unhappy. The only way they find meaningful happiness is when they are working, either for a living or for the benefit of their families. The novel demonstrates the importance of the Puritan work ethic, which dictates that it is holy to do work. This work ethic, in line with the transcendentalist teachings with which Alcott grew up, thrived in New England, where many Puritans lived and where the novel takes place. Alcott ultimately recommends work not as a means to a material end, but rather as a means to the expression of inner goodness and creativity through productivity.

THE IMPORTANCE OF BEING GENUINE

Little Women takes great pains to teach a lesson about the importance of being genuine. To make this point, Alcott contrasts the Marches with more well-to-do young women like Amy Moffat and Sally Gardiner. Transcendentalists emphasized the importance of paying more attention to the inner spiritual self than to temporary, earthly conditions like wealth and impressive appearances, and Alcott incorporates this philosophy into *Little Women.* For instance, Meg and Amy constantly struggle with vanity, and eventually overcome it. Amy turns down Fred Vaughn's offer of marriage, even though he is rich, because she does not love him. The March sisters all learn to be happy with their respective lots in life and not to yearn for meaningless riches. The Marches' snug New England home is presented as more desirable than mansions in Paris. This theme is particularly American, especially distinctive of New England. Unlike their counterparts in Europe, many middle-class Americans at the time did not mind having come from humble origins and did not crave titles or other superficial trappings of wealth. These Americans wanted only what they deserved and believed that what they deserved depended on how hard they worked.

MOTIFS

Motifs are recurring structures, contrasts, or literary devices that can help to develop and inform the text's major themes.

MUSIC

In *Little Women,* music has an interesting relationship to a character's degree of conformity. For the March girls, the more musically inclined a sister is, the more traditionally feminine and adherent to feminine duty she is. Marmee sings to the girls all the time, and she embodies the ideal dutiful and domestic mother. Beth, similarly, is both very musical and very passive. In contrast, Amy has a bad voice and Jo has the worst voice of all; both girls are independent and impatient with the limitations placed on women. Interestingly, Laurie also likes music and wants to be a professional musician, but this interest makes him ill-adapted to the role expected of him as a man.

TEACHING

Many of the characters in *Little Women* are teachers, reinforcing the idea that the novel is didactic and that we are supposed to learn from the novel's lessons. Mr. March, for example, is a minister, and he instructs his congregation. Marmee, a good transcendentalist mother, reinforces the teaching of her husband. Mr. Brooke and Professor Bhaer, two men whom March girls marry, are teachers by profession. In the end, Jo inherits Plumfield, Aunt March's house, and she and Bhaer turn it into a school for boys. The frequent interaction that the novel's characters have with teaching—

both giving and learning lessons—reflects the structured society in which they live.

DIFFERING USES OF LANGUAGE

Language appears throughout the novel in an interesting inverse relationship with creativity: the more proper the language one of the March girls uses, the less creative and independent she is. Beth does not talk much, for example, and Meg uses proper language; both are typically feminine women, and their relationship to language reflects their alignment with what society expects of them. In contrast, Jo swears and Amy mispronounces words. These two, the independent artists of the family, resist conforming to the behavior that society expects of them, including the use of proper and delicate speech.

SYMBOLS

Symbols are objects, characters, figures, or colors used to represent abstract ideas or concepts.

UMBRELLAS

In *Little Women,* umbrellas symbolize the protection a man offers a woman. Before Meg and John Brooke get married, Jo gets angry at Mr. Brooke's umbrella. It seems Jo is angry that Mr. Brooke is going to take care of her sister. At the end of the novel, Professor Bhaer extends his umbrella over Jo, and her acceptance of its coverage symbolizes that she is ready to accept not only his love and protection, but also the idea that men are supposed to offer women love and protection.

BURNING

Little Women is filled with images of burning that simultaneously represent writing, genius, and anger. At a party, Jo wears a dress with a burn mark on the back, which symbolizes her resistance to having to play a conventional female role. In anger, Amy burns Jo's manuscript after Jo will not let her come to a play. Whenever Jo writes, her family describes her inspiration as genius burning. At the end of the novel, Jo burns her sensationalist stories after Professor Bhaer criticizes that style of writing. This fire seems to destroy her earlier self as well, as it marks the end of the fiery Jo of the novel's beginning.

Summary & Analysis

SUMMARY & ANALYSIS

Preface–Chapter 5

Summary — Preface

Little Women is prefaced by an excerpt from John Bunyan's seventeenth-century novel *The Pilgrim's Progress,* an allegorical, or symbolic, novel about living a Christian life. The excerpt concerns the novel's female character, Mercy, not its main male character, Christian, indicating that Alcott's novel will be a guide for young girls.

Summary — Chapter 1: Playing Pilgrims

> *I'll try and be what he loves to call me, "a little*
> *woman," and not be rough and wild; but do my duty*
> *here instead of wanting to be somewhere else.*
> (See QUOTATIONS, p. 49)

One December evening in the mid-nineteenth century, the March girls—Meg, Jo, Beth, and Amy—sit at home, bewailing their poverty. The March family used to be wealthy, but Mr. March lost his money. This year, his daughters expect no Christmas presents. Meg admits to wanting presents anyway. Similarly, Jo, the bookworm, yearns for a copy of *Undine and Sintram,* a book of two German tales. Beth wants new music, and Amy sighs for drawing pencils. Meg, who works as a nanny, and Jo, who works as a companion to Aunt March, complain about their jobs. Meanwhile, Beth complains about having to do the housekeeping, and Amy complains that she does not have a nice nose.

The girls decide that they will each buy themselves a present in order to brighten their Christmas. Soon, however, they change their minds and resolve to buy presents for their mother, Marmee, instead. They then discuss Jo's play, "The Witch's Curse," which they will perform on Christmas Day. While they talk, Marmee comes home with a letter from Mr. March, who is serving as a Union chaplain in the Civil War. The letter reminds his little women to be good, which makes them feel ashamed of their earlier complaining. They resolve to bear their burdens more cheerfully. Meg's burden is her vanity, Jo's is her temper, Beth's is her housework, and Amy's is her selfishness. Marmee suggests that the sisters pretend they are playing pilgrims, a game from the girls' childhood in which they act out scenes from John Bunyan's didactic novel *The Pilgrim's Progress*. In this game, each girl shoulders a burden and tries to make her way to the Celestial City. Bunyan's novel and the game are both allegories of living a Christian life. The physical burdens stand for real-life burdens, and the Celestial City stands for heaven. The sisters agree to try the game again, but this time by practicing Christian values in their real lives. They all sing before bedtime.

SUMMARY — CHAPTER 2: A MERRY CHRISTMAS

On Christmas morning, the girls wake to find books under their pillows. Jo and Meg go downstairs to find Marmee, but the family servant, Hannah, tells her that Marmee has gone to aid poor neighbors. When Marmee returns, she asks her daughters to give their delicious Christmas breakfast to the starving Hummel family. The girls agree to do so and end up enjoying the good work they have done. That evening, they perform their play, in which Jo gets to play male roles. After the performance, the girls come downstairs to find a feast laid out on the table with fresh flowers and ice cream. Mr. Laurence, their neighbor, had heard of the family's charitable morning and sent the feast to reward their generosity. Jo wants to meet Mr. Laurence's grandson.

SUMMARY — CHAPTER 3: THE LAURENCE BOY

Jo reads in the attic with her pet rat, Scrabble, while eating apples. Meg comes to her and tells her that the two of them have been invited to a New Year's Eve party at the home of Meg's friend, Sallie Gardiner. Meg is very excited, but does not know what to wear. Unlike Meg, Jo is not particularly excited, but agrees to go anyway. Problems plague the girls as they get ready for the party. Jo burns Meg's hair while trying to curl it, and Meg decides to wear shoes that are too tight. Jo must wear a dress that is burned on the back, and she must hold her gloves balled up in her hand in order to hide the lemonade stains that cover them. Meg cares a great deal about social etiquette and has formed a code for her blundering sister: Meg tells Jo that she will raise her eyebrows at the party if Jo is doing anything improper, and she will nod if Jo is acting ladylike.

At the party, Jo hangs back, not knowing anyone. Finally, fearing that a boy is going to ask her to dance, Jo slips behind a curtain. There, she runs into her neighbor, the Laurence boy, who soon introduces himself as Laurie. The two chat and become very comfortable with each other. They dance, but out of the way of everyone else in order to hide Jo's dress. Meg sprains her ankle, and Laurie offers to take her and Jo home in his carriage. When they arrive home, Meg and Jo tell their younger sisters all about the party.

SUMMARY — CHAPTER 4: BURDENS

After the holiday festivities, the girls find going back to their jobs difficult. Meg does not want to look after the King children, whom she baby-sits, and Jo is reluctant to tend to Aunt March, for Aunt March makes Jo read boring books aloud. Though Aunt March is strict with Jo, Jo does like her; both women are stubborn and determined. Jo loves the book collection Uncle March left behind—she feels that it compensates for having to read to Aunt March.

The shyest March sister, Beth, stays home, does housework dutifully, and takes care of her doll collection, most of which is damaged in some way. Little Amy goes to school and grieves over her flat nose. The girls are all friends, but Amy is special to Meg, and Beth is special to Jo. When the sisters are finished with work, they tell stories from the day to entertain each other. Marmee gives a lecture on being grateful for one's blessings. Jo playfully quotes Aunt Chloe, a character from Harriet Beecher Stowe's novel *Uncle Tom's Cabin,* who urges her listeners to be grateful for their blessings.

SUMMARY — CHAPTER 5: BEING NEIGHBORLY

One winter afternoon, Jo goes outside to shovel a path in the snow. While she is outside, she sees Laurie in a window. She throws a snowball at the window to get his attention. Laurie leans out and tells Jo that he has been ill. Feeling sorry for him, Jo says she will go keep him company if it is all right with her mother. Marmee permits her to go, and Jo arrives at Laurie's house with food, kittens, and trinkets to make him feel better. They chat and laugh all afternoon. Laurie tells Jo that he is lonely and longs to be friends with her family. To Jo's delight, Laurie shows her his grandfather's library. When Laurie must leave to see the doctor, Jo stays in the room. Mr. Laurence comes in, and Jo, thinking he is Laurie, speaks somewhat disparagingly of a painting of Mr. Laurence. Luckily, Mr. Laurence enjoys Jo's candor, and they become fast friends. He invites Jo to stay for tea, feeling that this companionship is just what Laurie needs. After tea, Laurie plays the piano for Jo. This activity upsets Mr. Laurence, who does not want Laurie to pursue music. Jo goes home and tells her family all about the lovely day and the gorgeous house.

ANALYSIS — PREFACE–CHAPTER 5

Little Women begins with each of the March daughters making a statement that reveals her personality. With these differing statements, Alcott establishes the framework for an exploration into the different ways the girls grow up. Jo speaks first, showing that she is the most outspoken of the four. Meg's admission that she hates being poor reveals her tendency to be materialistic. Although she is a very virtuous girl, Meg craves luxury. Amy also loathes her poverty; she adores lovely things and wants to own them. The least selfish sister, Beth, often functions as the conscience of the group. Her happy remark that at least the girls have each other and their parents reveals that although Beth, like her sisters, wants what she does not have, she is content to count her blessings.

As Chapter 1 progresses, we learn more about the girls' individual tastes and quirks. Jo is a tomboy who "grabs the heels of her boots in a gentlemanly manner," teases Amy, and dreads the thought of being made to grow up and behave primly and properly. She longs to fight in the Civil War. Meg is motherly, gently reproving her sisters when they quarrel and complain. Beth is the loving peacemaker. Amy is charming and feminine, if vain and mannered.

Over the course of the novel, Alcott develops these girls as separate individuals. The obstacles they face are usually a result of their respective traits, and the trouble one sister faces would not have the same effect on another. Many critics have noted that Alcott's four girls are different from each other so that every reader may identify with at least one sister and glean some wisdom from that sister's blunders. Alcott's novel can thus be seen as a guide for her readers, just as *Pilgrim's Progress* is a guide for the March girls.

From the outset, Alcott explores the March girls' discomfort with their domestic situation. The novel begins with the four girls, their mother, and an absent father. The dissatisfaction the sisters feel at the beginning of the novel seems to stem just as much from the absence of their father as it does from the pangs of anticipating a poverty-stricken Christmas. The girls' desire for presents is not just materialistic. Their opening lines constitute direct and unusual statements of female desire. All of the March sisters want something greater than the limited existence that nineteenth-century society offers young women; they are not content to do the mundane chores appropriated to them.

Mr. March's letter inspires the girls to bear their burdens more calmly, illustrating that, from the outset, the March sisters' task is to become more humble, good, and dutiful. Alcott does not consider this project trifling, even though it occurs in a domestic sphere. By making her characters imitate *Pilgrim's Progress,* a novel in which the male character has grand adventures, Alcott elevates women's everyday lives and indicates that the struggles of ordinary women are as important as the struggles of adventuring men.

Jo is immediately characterized as the most adventuresome, independent sister. She resists the role of typical adult female and tries to carve out a separate space for herself as a different kind of woman. She writes her own plays and creates for herself new roles in which she can play the hero—the sort of role typically reserved for a male character. Jo's difference from her sisters and other women, however, is as isolating as it is freeing. Jo writes in the attic, apart from the rest of the family, as though she is trying to leave society. In her quest to flout society's rules for women, Jo must be spiritually alone, as symbolized by her physical isolation in the attic. Additionally, Jo wears a burned dress to the New Year's Eve ball; the dress, a symbol of traditional femininity, is marred by the burns, which symbolize Jo's own objections to traditional femininity.

When Jo discovers Laurie at the Gardiners' party, she finds a friend who is very similar to herself, especially in his nonconformity to gender roles. Jo hates her given name, Josephine, because she thinks it too feminine and "sentimental." Laurie dislikes his given name, Theodore, because his friends tease him and call him "Dora." Both Jo and Laurie instead take on androgynous nicknames that are not specifically male or female. Furthermore, just as Jo shies away from stereotypically feminine activities in favor of stereotypically masculine ones, Laurie pursues music, which was considered a feminine pursuit at the time, instead of business, the masculine activity his grandfather wishes him to pursue. Both Jo and Laurie thwart the gender stereotypes of their time and the expectations of their families. Because of their differences from other people and their similarities to one another, they seem to belong together.

CHAPTERS 6–10

SUMMARY — CHAPTER 6:
BETH FINDS THE PALACE BEAUTIFUL

The March girls start spending time at the Laurences' house. Meg loves to walk in the greenhouse there, and Amy loves to look at the artwork. Beth loves Mr. Laurence's piano, but she is still afraid of him; she will not venture far inside the house. Mr. Laurence learns of Beth's fears and comes over to the Marches' house one night, talking about how no one plays the piano and how no one is around the house during the day. With that assurance, Beth decides to venture into the house during the day and play the piano. Unbeknownst to her, Mr. Laurence sometimes leaves his door open to hear her play. Beth reminds him of his beloved granddaughter who passed away. After a while, Beth makes Mr. Laurence a pair of slippers to show her gratitude. In return, he sends her the little piano that his granddaughter owned, which thrills Beth. Jo tells Beth that she should go thank him, thinking that her shy sister would never be so bold. To everyone's surprise, Beth marches over to Mr. Laurence's house and kisses his cheek. The two have solidified a friendship.

SUMMARY — CHAPTER 7:
AMY'S VALLEY OF HUMILIATION

At Amy's school, the girls trade pickled limes, a fashionable treat at that time. Amy is worried because she has been given many limes but doesn't have the money to buy limes for her friends in return. Taking pity on her little sister, Meg gives Amy money to buy some limes. Amy tells her enemy, a girl named Miss Snow, that she will not get any limes. In revenge, Miss Snow tells the teacher, who has forbidden limes in class, of Amy's hoard. The teacher makes Amy throw the limes out the window, strikes her on the palm, and makes her stand at the front of the classroom until recess. At recess, Amy goes home and tells her family what happened. They are not sorry for her punishment, for she did wrong, but they are upset that she was struck on the palm. Marmee decides that Amy may have a vacation from school and learn at home with Beth.

Summary — Chapter 8: Jo Meets Apollyon

I am angry nearly every day of my life.
(See QUOTATIONS, p. 50)

Jo and Meg are going to a play with Laurie, and Amy wants to go too. Jo tells her, a bit harshly, that she cannot go because she was not invited. Angered, Amy tells Jo that Jo will be sorry. During the play, Jo feels some remorse for her bad treatment of her little sister. When the older girls arrive home, Amy gives Jo the cold shoulder. The next day, Jo finds her manuscript missing, and discovers that Amy has burned it. Jo says she will never forgive Amy, because that book was her pride and joy. Amy apologizes, and Marmee warns Jo not to "let the sun go down upon [her] anger," but Jo is not ready to forgive Amy. The next afternoon, Jo and Laurie go skating, and Amy tries to follow. Laurie warns Jo that the ice is thin in the middle, but Jo does not pass on the message to Amy. Amy falls through the ice, and Jo hesitates for a moment, paralyzed with fear. Finally, Laurie comes to Amy's rescue. At home, Jo confesses to Marmee that her anger overwhelms her. Marmee admits that she too struggles with controlling a quick temper. Jo is amazed and bolstered by this revelation, for she has always seen Marmee as a perfectly calm person. Amy and Jo end their quarrel and make up.

Summary — Chapter 9: Meg Goes to Vanity Fair

I'd rather see you poor men's wives, if you were
happy, beloved, contented, than queens on thrones,
without self-respect and peace.
(See QUOTATIONS, p. 51)

Meg has plans to stay with Annie Moffat, a wealthy friend. She packs all of her nicest clothes, but wishes she had more splendid attire. The Moffats are very fashionable. While Meg is there, they visit friends, go to plays, and give parties. At the first party, Meg wears her simple clothes, and she hears people gossiping that Meg's mother must be intending for Meg to marry Laurie for his money. At the next party, the Moffat girls insist on dressing Meg in borrowed finery. She is a bit embarrassed about the luxury of her attire, but she enjoys playing the role of a fashionable girl. Laurie is at the party and reprimands Meg for being so frivolous. His criticism makes Meg regret letting her friends dress her. When Meg gets home, she tells Marmee and Jo how she dressed up and overheard gossip about herself and Laurie. Marmee tells them that she has no such plans for Meg. She says that she hopes only that the girls are happy in youth and in marriage, and that they are good. She adds that she hopes that they understand that appearances are shallow and that true love is built on something deeper than money.

SUMMARY — CHAPTER 10: THE P.C. AND P.O.

In the spring, the girls take to gardening. They also hold meetings of the Pickwick Club, a society for arts and letters modeled on an all-male society in Charles Dickens's novel *The Pickwick Papers*. The sisters produce a newsletter each week, with advertisements, poems, and stories. At one meeting, Jo proposes that they invite Laurie to join. At first, Amy and Meg are horrified; they do not want a boy making fun of them. As soon as they give in, Laurie bursts out of the closet where he has been hiding. He presents the club with a postal box to be put between the houses so that the March sisters and Laurie may pass things back and forth.

ANALYSIS — CHAPTERS 6–10

In these second five chapters, each girl marks a step on her journey from childhood to adulthood by struggling and succeeding in overcoming a fault. First, Beth must overcome her shyness in order to pursue her musical hobby. She is rewarded for her efforts with a piano, and she proves that her gratitude trumps her shyness when she marches across to Mr. Laurence's house and gives him a kiss in thanks. Beth's attachment to Mr. Laurence also symbolizes that she is the most old-fashioned of the sisters—the most eager to play traditional female roles for an old patriarch, a male figure at the head of a household. Though Mr. Laurence is a benevolent presence, he also symbolizes oppressive male behavior, for he does not let Laurie follow his dream of becoming a musician, a culturally feminine pursuit; instead, he wants Laurie to be a real man with a professional career in business. His earlier rewarding of the Marches' selflessness on Christmas with a feast reinforces the gender stereotype of the perpetually giving, selfless woman who is taken care of by a man.

In Chapter 7, Amy is too concerned with the humiliation and unfairness of her punishment to worry about the crime that brings on the punishment. She is preoccupied with appearances. When her mother chides her for being arrogant, Amy absorbs the lecture and understands it. She speaks admiringly of the fact that Laurie is both accomplished and modest, and we understand that she has realized the value of being humble. As she says, "It's nice to have accomplishments, and be elegant; but not to show off." Amy is more vain and difficult than her other sisters, but Alcott characterizes these flaws as partly charming, and certainly as the product of Amy's young age. Alcott suggests that Amy's heart is in the right place, and that she has the capacity to improve.

Jo's anger at the destruction of her writing, the art with which she tries to transcend the limitations placed on her gender, is portrayed as understandable but also dangerous. It is understandable that Jo would be furious with Amy, but it is dangerous that Jo lets her anger take over. Nevertheless, Jo's anger is an essential aspect of her character. Similarly, Marmee's admission that "I am angry nearly every day of my life" reveals that anger is an essential component of her character, as well. Critics often point out the feminist underpinnings of such an admission: Alcott may be suggesting that women—even wise, patient mothers—are, or have a right to be, angered by the oppression they suffer.

In Chapter 9, Meg's attraction to the luxury of Annie Moffat's life and subsequent longing for finery and riches of her own sets her up as an example of how materialistic desires can corrupt a good person. Laurie's disapproving lecture at the ball reminds Meg that she should not put on airs or pretend to be someone she is not. Throughout *Little Women,* Alcott condemns judging people by their exteriors, telling us that it is not shameful to be poor or to be a woman. The importance Alcott places on the mind and soul—people's interiors—reflects transcendental values.

The fact that the sisters mimic the all-male society of Dickens's novel is characterized as humorous, but the club's activities highlight the limited role available to women in nineteenth-century America. The announcements in the newspaper the girls produce are revealing: the first relates that a "Strong-Minded Lecturer," a woman named Miss Oranthy Bluggage, will give a talk on "Woman and Her Position;" and the last mentions a lauded new play, presumably written by Jo. These strong feminist announcements are balanced by announcements for a cooking class, "The Dustpan Society," and doll's clothes. Although the tone of these announcements is comical, Alcott seems to be making the point that for the March sisters, traditional women's work and more unconventional womanly strength exist side by side. Moreover, Alcott pokes fun at her own rather moralizing, oversimplifying depiction of the sisters in the section of the newspaper labeled "Weekly Report," which reads simply: "Meg—Good. Jo—Bad. Beth—Very good. Amy—Middling." For readers who might scoff at the simplistic, one-dimensional portrayal of the girls, the Weekly Report is Alcott's humorous admission of her own authorial choices.

CHAPTERS 11–15

SUMMARY — CHAPTER 11: EXPERIMENTS

During the summer, the King family, for whom Meg is the governess, and Aunt March go on vacation, leaving Meg and Jo free from their duties. Relieved, Meg and Jo decide to do nothing at all with their newfound freedom. The younger girls, Amy and Beth, also take a break from their studies. After the girls neglect their chores for almost a week, Marmee and Hannah take a day off as well. That day, the girls fail miserably at running the household smoothly. They soon discover that Marmee has taught them a lesson about the importance of everyone doing at least a little work.

SUMMARY — CHAPTER 12: CAMP LAURENCE

One July day, Meg receives one glove in the postbox, though she has lost them both and wonders where its mate is. With the glove comes a German song translated by Mr. Brooke, Laurie's tutor. Laurie has also sent an invitation to a picnic to be held the next day. The following day, the March girls attend the picnic along with various other guests: Sallie Gardiner; Ned Moffat, Annie Moffat's older brother; Mr. Brooke; Laurie's British friends, Fred and Kate Vaughn; and their siblings, Frank and Grace Vaughn. During the picnic, Fred cheats in a game of cricket. Jo notices and is annoyed, but manages to control her temper. When Kate discovers that Meg works as a lowly governess, Kate is first rude and then patronizing. Mr. Brooke defends Meg, which leads to a long conversation between him and Meg. Meanwhile, Grace and Amy chat about ponies and Europe, and Beth has a conversation with Frank, who has a hurt leg. As the party breaks up, even the condescending Kate says that American girls are nice.

SUMMARY — CHAPTER 13: CASTLES IN THE AIR

> *I think I shall write books, and get rich and famous;*
> *that would suit me, so that is my favorite dream.*
> (See QUOTATIONS, p. 52)

Laurie swings idly on his hammock and spies the March girls walking out to a hill. There, the sisters sit working—knitting, sewing, drawing, and reading. Feeling left out, Laurie asks if he may join them. They admit him under the condition that he contribute something useful, as is consistent with the work ethic of the girls' Busy Bee Society. Laurie's contribution is his reading of a book to the sisters. While they work, all five friends discuss their dreams. Laurie wants to become a famous musician, Jo a famous author, and Amy a famous artist. Meg wants to be rich so that she does not have to work, and Beth wants everyone to be happy and together. Upset that Laurie cannot follow his dream, Jo tells him to run away from his grandfather, who does not want him to be a musician. Sensible Meg tells Laurie to ignore Jo's advice and to be good to both his grandfather and Mr. Brooke. Laurie decides to follow Meg's advice.

SUMMARY — CHAPTER 14: SECRETS

Jo finishes the manuscripts for two stories and brings them to a newspaperman in town without telling anyone. She is very anxious. She meets Laurie as she comes out of the news office. After he pleads with her to tell him what is going on, she confides her secret. Laurie then tells Jo his secret—that Mr. Brooke has kept Meg's glove and carries it with him wherever he goes. This secret disgusts Jo, because she hates the idea of someone loving Meg and taking her away. Laurie, in an attempt to cheer Jo, persuades her to race him down a hill. In a wild, messy state, they encounter Meg, who has just visited the Gardiners. Meg reprimands Jo, though she secretly feels tempted to join their romp. For about a week, Jo behaves strangely. Then, one day, she reads a story aloud from a paper and announces at the end that the story was hers. She has not gotten paid, but she says that she will for future stories. She feels wonderfully independent.

SUMMARY — CHAPTER 15: A TELEGRAM

November arrives, and everyone is glum. Marmee receives a telegram saying that Mr. March is ill and that she must go to Washington, D.C. to be with him. Marmee sends Laurie to ask Aunt March for money and sends Beth to ask Mr. Laurence for wine. In the spirit of the moment, Jo runs out to find a way to contribute. Later, Mr. Laurence offers Mr. Brooke as a travel companion for Marmee, and she gratefully accepts Mr. Brooke's company. Jo returns home, having earned twenty-five dollars by selling her hair. Pretty Amy is horrified that Jo has lost her "one beauty." Jo, however, is not sad until late at night, when she cries a little for her lost hair.

Analysis — Chapters 11–15

In Chapter 11, Alcott stresses the importance of work and suggests that idleness does not lead to happiness. Alcott has held up domestic work—such as cleaning the house, teaching young children, and nursing the sick—not as a particularly challenging or rewarding endeavor for women, but rather as an unfortunate duty. However, here she shows us that idleness is an inadequate alternative.

Alcott stresses the importance of work again in Chapter 12, indicating that it is a particularly American value. In this chapter, Kate Vaughn, Laurie's British friend, is set up as a foil, or contrast, to Meg. While both women are intelligent and attractive, Kate, the lady of leisure, is characterized as snobby, insensitive, and unkind. Meg, on the other hand, is unpretentious, sweet-natured, and hardworking.

At the beginning of Chapter 13, Laurie feels bad that the March sisters have left him out of their Busy Bee Society. Scholar Nina Auerbach feels that this scene indicates that a society of women can be complete without men; Laurie wants to join the women, not the other way around. Auerbach believes that *Little Women* often depicts an all-female world as paradise.

In Chapter 13, when the March girls and Laurie describe their goals, Jo, Laurie, and Amy stand apart from the rest of the group. They all have big, ambitious dreams, and none of them mentions marriage as a goal. Beth and Meg, however, have begun the process of conforming to the typical roles of the time: Meg, always conventional, wants a husband and a household of her own, while Beth typifies the perfect nineteenth-century woman in that she is "perfectly satisfied" and has no desires. Alcott may have drawn this chapter title, "Castles in the Air," from Henry David Thoreau's *Walden Pond,* an important transcendentalist work that advocates building castles in the air—dreaming, that is—and then building the foundations under them. Alcott suggests that Jo, Amy, and Laurie have built their castles in the air, but are prevented by gender roles from building foundations under them. Already, by the end of the chapter, Laurie has agreed to give up the feminine pursuit of music in order to pursue his grandfather's dreams for him.

In Chapter 14, Meg and Jo begin maturing into two very different types of women, as reflected in the difference between the role that each chooses for herself. Meg waits for her future to come to her, while becoming a more proper, elegant lady. Jo becomes independent through her work, both in terms of her income and her creativity. She leaves the protective shelter of the house and ventures out into the male world of newspapers. Jo even cuts off her hair, erasing her own femininity, in order to fulfill the stereotypically male role of providing money for the family.

CHAPTERS 16–20

SUMMARY — CHAPTER 16: LETTERS

Marmee departs, and the girls communicate with her by letter. The girls write letters in their own ways: Meg writes of everyday events in a refined way; Jo writes impassioned letters with slang and silly poems; Beth sends simple notes of love; and Amy strives for sophistication but ends up discussing trivialities. Hannah writes misspelled letters about home life, while Laurie writes short, humorous tidbits, and Mr. Laurence writes informative and sincere notes.

SUMMARY — CHAPTER 17: LITTLE FAITHFUL

For a while, the girls are extremely diligent in their work, but they soon grow lazy again. Marmee had asked her daughters to visit the Hummels every day, but Beth is the only one who has done so. One day, Beth asks that another sister take a turn visiting the Hummels, but her sisters, wrapped up in their own pursuits, ignore her. Finally, when no one else will go, Beth goes again. When she returns home, she tells Jo that the Hummel baby has just died from scarlet fever. She says that she feels strange and fears that she might have the disease too. Luckily, Jo and Meg have had it already, so they are not in danger of contracting the illness if Beth does in fact have it. Hannah decides that Dr. Bangs should be sent for to look at Beth. He arrives and says that she shows symptoms of the disease. The family decides to send Amy to Aunt March's, since Amy is susceptible to scarlet fever, but she will not go until Laurie promises that he will come visit her every day. At

Aunt March's, Amy is harassed by her aunt's speaking parrot and finds herself miserable.

SUMMARY — CHAPTER 18: DARK DAYS
Beth is much more seriously ill than anyone supposed. After a while, the family decides that Marmee must be sent for, just in case something dreadful happens. Jo breaks down in front of Laurie, saying that she does not want Beth to die. Laurie admits that he telegraphed for Marmee the day before and that she will be arriving that night. Around two in the morning, Jo and Meg notice a change in Beth: the fever and pained look are gone. Jo whispers goodbye to her sister. Hannah, however, announces that the fever has broken. Beth is not dying but rather recovering. The doctor confirms the good news, and Marmee arrives.

SUMMARY — CHAPTER 19: AMY'S WILL
During Beth's illness, Amy has a hard time living with Aunt March. Though Aunt March likes Amy, she makes her niece work very hard. For consolation, Amy turns to the servant, Esther, who tells her stories and plays with her among Aunt March's old dresses and jewelry. After a while, Esther tells Amy that she finds solace in prayer. She even tells Amy that she will help set up a small shrine for her. Esther then reveals that Amy is to receive her aunt's turquoise ring. From then on, Amy behaves extremely well so as to be assured of getting the ring. She and Esther set up a chapel in a dressing closet, and Amy derives comfort from praying there. Amy also decides to make a will, in case she falls ill and dies. She has Esther and Laurie serve as witnesses.

SUMMARY — CHAPTER 20: CONFIDENTIAL
Marmee watches carefully over Beth, while Laurie goes to Aunt March's to tell Amy of Beth's recovery. Later, Marmee also comes to visit Amy. Amy shows her the chapel, which Marmee approves of as a place for quiet reflection. Amy also asks Marmee if she may wear the turquoise ring that Aunt March has now given her. She wants to wear it to remind herself not to be selfish, and Marmee approves of this plan. When Marmee gets home, Jo tells her that Mr. Brooke has Meg's glove. Marmee asks Jo if she thinks Meg cares for Mr. Brooke and tells Jo that Mr. Brooke has confessed an interest in Meg. This unwelcome revelation saddens Jo, who does not want to lose Meg. Marmee says that she too would like Meg to remain in the house until

she is at least twenty years old. Jo says that she wanted Meg to marry Laurie and live in luxury. Meg comes in, and Marmee evaluates how Meg reacts to discussion of Mr. Brooke. She decides that Meg does not love him yet but that she will learn to love him soon.

ANALYSIS — CHAPTERS 16–20

In several ways, Chapter 16 reinforces the idea that the mother is the emotional and practical head of the family. Alcott portrays Marmee's absence in Chapter 16 as much more significant than Mr. March's absence throughout the whole novel thus far. The family, which has managed perfectly well without the father's presence, struggles as soon as the mother leaves. The girls cry over Marmee's departure, suggesting that their father's continuing grave illness does not cause them as much anxiety as Marmee's initial absence. Though a letter from Mr. March is read early in the novel, no letters from the girls to him are ever described. In contrast, an entire chapter is devoted to the girls' letters to their mother. Female-female bonds are strong in the novel, and most female-male bonds are weak by comparison.

Alcott places blame for Beth's illness both on selfishness and on selflessness. Certainly, we are meant to condemn Beth's sisters for their selfish refusal to visit the Hummels. In one way, Meg and Jo are responsible for Beth's grave illness, because they are immune from scarlet fever; if they had visited the Hummels instead of Beth, no one would have gotten sick. It is no coincidence that on the very day Beth asks them to go to the Hummels in her stead and they refuse, she falls ill. Alcott positions these events in a cause and effect relationship, which places blame squarely on the shoulders of Meg and Jo. At the same time, though, one can argue that Beth's selflessness is responsible for her illness. Scholar Elizabeth Lennox Keyser has suggested that Beth's illness is symbolic of her being the weakest, most conforming March sister. In condemning selflessness, Alcott is probably condemning not Beth but rather a society that idealizes women who put everyone else above themselves. Beth is the most stereotypically ideal sister, and it is she who falls ill. Extreme selflessness is presented as both admirable and potentially dangerous.

In Chapter 18, Amy matures by leaps and bounds at Aunt March's house. She confronts her selfishness, realizing with shame that she is more worried about getting her hands on the turquoise ring than she is about her ill sister. She learns that a place for quiet reflection is often necessary; she even thinks seriously about death, demonstrating that she can overcome material concerns. She does not lose her aesthetic values, however—her chapel, after all, is beautiful and dramatic, and her reminder not to be selfish is her turquoise ring. Her continued appreciation of beautiful objects here suggests that while she is becoming an adult, she is still a child at heart.

That Amy writes out a will, leaving her treasured possessions to her beloved family and friends, demonstrates her ability to blend generosity with regard for material things. On the one hand, Amy's attachment to things of the earth suggests that she has not fully absorbed the transcendentalist values mastered by Beth, who, though close to death, never thinks of making a will. On the other hand, Alcott suggests that Amy has something equally important that Beth lacks: the will to live and thrive. We must decide which way of thinking about the world is better or more admirable.

CHAPTERS 21–23

SUMMARY — CHAPTER 21:
LAURIE MAKES MISCHIEF, AND JO MAKES PEACE

Jo has trouble keeping secret the potential courtship between Meg and Mr. Brooke. Laurie tries to get the secret out of Jo and grows annoyed when he cannot. In the meantime, Meg receives a letter allegedly from Mr. Brooke declaring his love. She answers it before Jo gets a chance to tell her that Laurie probably wrote it. The reply from Mr. Brooke says that he has never written a love letter. Jo says that she thinks Laurie wrote this letter and the earlier one with the glove. Sure enough, Laurie comes over, confesses, and apologizes. Meg and Jo tell him never to reveal the story to anyone. Laurie leaves, and Jo decides to let him know that she is not angry with him. She goes over to the Laurence house, where Laurie is in a terrible mood. His grandfather has demanded to know what is bothering Laurie; Laurie has refused to tell him, and they have quarreled. Upset, Laurie tells Jo he wants to run away. In order to help, Jo explains Laurie's actions to his grandfather, who writes a note of apology to his grandson.

SUMMARY — CHAPTER 22: PLEASANT MEADOWS

Christmas arrives and everyone is very merry. Laurie and Jo make a snowwoman for Beth, and everyone else gets lovely presents too.

The Laurences and Mr. Brooke surprise the family by bringing Mr. March home for Christmas. They have a very joyful time, and Mr. March tells the girls how much each of them has grown up. Jo is upset, however, because she can feel Meg slipping away from the family in her preoccupation with Mr. Brooke.

SUMMARY — CHAPTER 23:
AUNT MARCH SETTLES THE QUESTION

Meg becomes nervous and blushes whenever Mr. Brooke is mentioned. Her parents think that she is too young to be married, and in order to follow their wishes, she prepares a speech of rejection in case he makes advances. When Mr. Brooke comes over, she softens somewhat in his presence. Nevertheless, when he professes his love for her, she tells him she is too young. Aunt March arrives in the middle of this encounter. Mr. Brooke steps out, and Aunt March lectures Meg, telling her she should marry someone wealthy. Aunt March's tirade makes Meg defend her right to love and marry Mr. Brooke. After Aunt March leaves, Mr. Brooke comes back into the room, confessing that he has heard Meg's conversation. Meg says that she did not realize how much she admired Mr. Brooke until she had to defend him. He is thrilled by her realization and asks her to marry him in a few years. Meg agrees, and her parents consent. Jo is unhappy because she feels that she is losing her sister. Laurie arrives with Mr. Laurence, and they are both thrilled for the new couple. The first part of the book ends with the family gathered in the living room.

ANALYSIS — CHAPTERS 21–23

Meg does a lot of growing up in these three chapters; she falls in love and becomes engaged. Despite the outward happiness the family expresses for Meg's impending marriage, a negative current runs beneath the surface of the affair. Jo abhors losing a sister, and often likens Meg's love for Mr. Brooke to a disease. In Chapter 21, Jo says of Meg, "She feels it in the air—love, I mean—and she's going very fast. She's got most of the symptoms, is twittery and cross, don't eat, lies awake, and mopes in corners." In the wake of Beth's recent recovery from grave illness, Jo's metaphors about love as a sickness seem more serious than comical. Alcott may want her readers to draw a connection between Beth's and Meg's conditions; both girls are stuck in unhealthy nineteenth-century female roles. Beth is struck down by the selflessness that is encouraged in women, and

Meg is struck down—at least in Jo's opinion—by agreeing to become a typical wife.

On the other hand, when Meg agrees to marry Mr. Brooke, she demonstrates that at last she has overcome her own weakness for luxury and riches. John is not a rich man, and he will not provide Meg with the glamorous lifestyle she once coveted, but she loves him nonetheless. Alcott underlines Meg's triumphant victory over materialism by having Aunt March object to Mr. Brooke's poverty, and then letting us hear Meg's passionate defense of him and her insistence that his poverty does not matter because he is a good man and they love each other

Still, Alcott does not entirely gloss over the issue of poverty. *Little Women* presents a less idealized version of domesticity than many earlier novels. Her characters have real financial problems, and she suggests that Meg is being sweetly naïve to think that money will make no difference to her happiness. She suggests that the best type of marriage—as in the novels of the nineteenth-century English author Jane Austen—combines both love and money, since the conventions of nineteenth-century society make it difficult, if not impossible, for women to earn their own livings.

The end of this chapter marks the close of Part One. Part One was published on its own, and, when it was well-received, Alcott went on to write and publish Part Two. She ends this first part somewhat artificially, saying that "the curtain falls upon Meg, Jo, Beth and Amy." By mentioning a curtain close, Alcott calls attention to the fact that the story she is presenting to us is artificial and constructed. She seems to acknowledge that her novel has grown more conventional and romantic and less real—as though we are watching a play, with characters that are obviously fictional.

CHAPTERS 24–28

SUMMARY — CHAPTER 24: GOSSIP

This chapter, the first in Part Two of the novel, opens after three years have passed. Meg is about to get married. The war has ended, and Mr. March has returned home. Mr. Brooke has gone to war too, and has returned with only a minor injury. In the meantime, Meg has learned more about keeping house, and Amy has taken over Jo's job caring for Aunt March. Jo has continued to write stories for the newspaper, for which she is paid one dollar a column, while Laurie has passed the years at college. Many of Laurie's college friends fall in love with Amy, who has blossomed into a lovely young woman. Sallie Gardiner has married Ned Moffat. As Meg's wedding nears, the March women all work on Meg's new little house. Laurie comes home with gifts for Meg, and Jo tells him that he spends too much money. To Jo's dismay, Laurie tells Jo that, whether she likes it or not, she will be the next one to marry.

SUMMARY — CHAPTER 25: THE FIRST WEDDING

Meg's wedding is casual and small. In their summer dresses, all of the March girls look beautiful and slightly different from how they appeared three years ago: Jo is a bit softened, Amy is gorgeous, and Beth is pale and fragile but good-spirited. The wedding goes smoothly. When Laurie asks what happened to the expensive wine that his grandfather sent, Meg tells him that they have put a little aside for medicinal use and have given the rest away. Meg then asks Laurie never to drink alcohol. He agrees to her request. After the celebration, Meg leaves, asking her family members to keep her in their hearts.

SUMMARY — CHAPTER 26: ARTISTIC ATTEMPTS

Amy spends much time working on her art. Though she is not a genius, she has passion. At the end of one of her art classes, she asks Marmee if she can invite her girlfriends over for a luncheon and an afternoon of sketching. She wants to make the party elaborate and lovely, and she offers to pay for all of it. Marmee consents, but only in order to teach Amy a lesson about trying to present herself as something she is not. The party ends up costing more than Amy plans. She must reschedule the picnic because it is rainy and set up everything again the next day. When she goes out to buy lobster, she runs into a friend of Laurie's. He sees the lobster, which was considered low-class food at the time, and she is very embarrassed, although she manages to recover and charm him. Finally, the party begins, but only one person shows up. During the party, Amy is delightful and merry, but she is very disappointed at the way things have turned out. Her family is very kind and tactful.

SUMMARY — CHAPTER 27: LITERARY LESSONS

Jo continues to write. Then, one night, she goes to a lecture on pyramids. While she is waiting for the lecture to begin, a boy shows her a newspaper. It has a sensationalist story that Jo finds silly. She sees that the newspaper is offering a one hundred dollar prize for the best sensationalist story. Excited, Jo writes a story, submits it, and wins. With the money, she sends Marmee and Beth to the seashore for several weeks to improve Beth's health. Jo keeps writing. She makes more money, providing for herself and the family. Finally, she decides to finish her novel, which is a romance. The publisher tells her to cut it down, and, after long consideration, she does. When the novel is published, it earns her $300, as well as mixed reviews from critics.

SUMMARY — CHAPTER 28: DOMESTIC EXPERIENCES

Meg learns to tend house and be a good wife. She and Mr. Brooke must be careful with money because they are poor. One day, Meg tries to make jelly, which turns out to be a miserable failure. That night, John brings home unexpected company. Meg gets angry at his insensitivity, even though she has told him that he can bring home guests anytime he wants. They have their first fight, but soon make up. The next trial comes when Meg is frivolous and spends too much money shopping with Sallie Gardiner. She buys expensive fabric, which prohibits John from getting a new coat. Meg asks Sallie to buy the fabric from her, which Sallie does, and Meg purchases a coat for John. Soon Meg becomes pregnant and gives birth to twins, John Laurence and Margaret, who are called Demi and Daisy for short.

ANALYSIS — CHAPTERS 24–28

Alcott began Chapter 24 after hearing feedback about Part One from her readers, publishers, and family. In order to satisfy a large reading public, she tries to please her readers, but often it is evident that she does not condone their tastes. Chapter 24, "Gossip," begins in a slightly flippant tone, mimicking the tone of Meg's rich friends and indicating that Alcott may herself be critical of the way in which her novel continues.

Amy continues to desire a more luxurious life, and she spends time and money attempting to impress the rich girls from her art class with a fancy party. As usual, the failure of her party provides the opportunity for Amy to learn a lesson about pretending to be something she is not. Alcott stresses that women living in poverty should hold fast to their dignity. She considers living beyond one's means extremely undignified, since the people one tries to impress by doing so can see through this facade and can recognize poverty and pretending for what they are. Dignity is only attainable, Alcott suggests, by accepting one's financial situation gracefully and refusing to be embarrassed by it.

Jo continues to develop into an independent woman. It is perhaps significant that when she goes to the lecture on the pyramids, she sits behind two women discussing women's rights. Although Jo does not discuss women's rights directly, she does believe that she can do anything she likes, even if that means foregoing the traditional woman's role as housewife. Jo revels in her independence and in her ability to provide financially for herself and her family. The whole family also supports her in her pursuits. Alcott quietly emphasizes the responsibility Jo bears. Her father urges her to wait for her book to ripen before she publishes it, but the unsavory truth of the matter is that the family desperately needs money, and Mr. March is doing little to provide it. Jo decides to sacrifice artistic ideals in order to provide for her family, and Alcott supports her in this endeavor.

In contrast to Amy and Jo, Meg submits wholeheartedly to being a good wife and homemaker. But her lapses into desire for luxury remind her that, married or not, she is still growing up. Alcott portrays marriage realistically, not as the happily-ever-after end of the story, but as one step in a lifetime, a step that does not drastically change the personality of either husband or wife. This realistic portrayal of marriage is heightened by the fact that Meg's wedding, though a happy event, breaks up the cozily cloistered feeling of Part One of the novel. The realities of life are setting in, and, perhaps sadly, the sisters have begun to scatter.

CHAPTERS 29–33

SUMMARY — CHAPTER 29: CALLS

Amy and Jo go out visiting, and Amy makes Jo dress up and behave nicely. At the first house, Amy reprimands Jo for being too reserved and for hardly speaking at all. To tease her sister, Jo imitates a social butterfly named May Chester at the second house they visit. Amy grows even more mortified as Jo reveals secrets of their poverty. At the third house, after Amy tells her to stop this new behavior, Jo amuses herself by playing with a group of young boys, telling them stories. As Amy and Jo walk to Aunt March's house, Amy declares that poor young women should be pleasant because they have nothing else to give. Disagreeing, Jo says that she will probably be crotchety all of her days. Aunt Carrol is at Aunt March's house when they arrive. During the visit, Amy is charming, but Jo is curt. Alcott indicates that something good will happen to Amy because she is so delightful that day.

SUMMARY — CHAPTER 30: CONSEQUENCES

Amy is to work at the art table at the Chesters' upcoming fair. She works hard to put the display together. The night before the fair, Mrs. Chester hears how the March girls insulted her daughter, May, and tells Amy that she should work at the flower table instead, while May will work at the art table. Amy is insulted, but she maintains her composure, taking her art with her to the new booth. The next day, hoping to smooth things over, Amy offers her art back to May. Over the course of the day, few people go to the flower table. That night, however, the Marches send over a brigade of young men led by Laurie. These boys surround Amy and buy all her flowers. Then, to kill May with kindness, Amy sends the boys to May's booth to buy the vases that May has made. Amy returns home to find the vases filled with flowers for her. She then receives a note from Aunt Carrol, telling her that she is going to Europe and wants Amy to accompany her. Amy is thrilled, but Jo is very disappointed, having hoped that she would get to go on the trip. Before Amy sails for Europe, she asks Laurie to come comfort her if something should happen. He agrees to do so.

SUMMARY — CHAPTER 31:
OUR FOREIGN CORRESPONDENT

Amy sends several letters from Europe, detailing her romps through England, France, Germany, and Switzerland. She says that she is trying to absorb every beautiful attraction. Along the way, she runs into Fred and Frank Vaughn, Laurie's English friends. She and Florence, Aunt Carrol's daughter, spend a lot of time with them, and it becomes clear that Fred is interested in courting Amy. She decides that she will accept him if he proposes. She is not madly in love with him, but she likes him and thinks that his fortune will help the whole family. But Fred finds out that Frank is very ill, and must leave abruptly. Fred asks Amy to remember him, and tells her meaningfully that he will return to her soon.

SUMMARY — CHAPTER 32: TENDER TROUBLES

Marmee asks Jo to find out if something is troubling Beth, for Beth's spirits seem low. After thinking, Jo concludes that Beth might be in love with Laurie, but Jo is afraid that Laurie is in love Jo herself. Jo asks her mother if she might go away for a while in an attempt to broaden her horizons and to escape Laurie's growing love. She hopes that Laurie will fall in love with Beth while she is gone. Marmee agrees that Jo and Laurie are unsuited for each other because they are too similar, with their strong wills and frequent quarrels. Jo decides to go to New York to live with a woman named Mrs. Kirke and to teach her children. When Jo tells Laurie of her decision to leave, he responds by telling her, teasingly but seriously, that she will not get out of his grasp so easily.

SUMMARY — CHAPTER 33: JO'S JOURNAL

Jo sends letters from New York. She reports that the children are fine and that she is enjoying her little room in the big boarding house. She also writes about another boarder, a German professor named Frederick Bhaer. Professor Bhaer does not have much money, and tutors children in order to make a living. He is not particularly good-looking, and is around forty years old. Jo watches him doing good for everyone around him and is impressed by his kindness. They become friends when she mends some of his garments for him. Soon, he begins teaching her German. At Christmas, he gives her a beloved volume of Shakespeare from which he hopes she will learn. She gives him many trinkets in return. For New Year's Eve, the boarding house has a masquerade, and Jo goes as Mrs. Malaprop, a character from a Restoration comedy by Richard Sheridan called *The Rivals*. Bhaer goes as Nick Bottom, from Shakespeare's *A Midsummer Night's Dream*. Jo thoroughly enjoys herself.

ANALYSIS — CHAPTERS 29–33

In Part Two of the novel, Alcott uses a narrative technique slightly different from the one she employs in Part One. Whereas the first part of the novel is didactic, tending to teach us lessons, the second part is sentimental, tending to steer the novel in an emotionally satisfying direction. Alcott addresses her audience more frequently here than she does in the first part; this direct address is a common device in sentimental literature. These direct and sometimes syrupy appeals to the reader are supposed to inspire emotion. This shift in genres may be due partly to audience response and artistic choices. It may also be due to the fact that Alcott is no longer writing about the cloistered, all-female household that so closely mimics her own early womanhood, but now writes about strictly imagined events. In particular, Jo's resemblance to Alcott lessens in the second part of the novel.

Amy's departure from America signals a departure from the everyday, humble life that she has led until now. She develops into a woman, learning to balance virtue and luxury. She adores being a part of wealthy society, but realizes that she does not want to lose the lessons she has learned from Marmee. If Alcott's idealization of Beth suggests that humility is the highest virtue, her portrayal of Amy suggests something different. She does not fault Amy for her love of luxury; rather, Alcott shows that Amy can both remain a good person and live a life of material wealth. She does not condemn Amy or punish her with dire consequences for her desire to own nice things and have elegant experiences. The fair provides a microcosm of Amy's ability to have it all: while participating in a high-class pursuit, she keeps the moral high ground. Amy may take her love of money too far, though; it remains to be seen whether Fred Vaughn is a morally acceptable candidate for marriage, given that Amy does not love him. Alcott suggests, however, that Amy is put in this slightly distasteful situation because she has a natural urge to help her own family out of its poverty. Alcott seems to insinuate that poverty makes morally ambiguous behavior acceptable if the motive behind such behavior is to alleviate that poverty.

Loving, charming, and rich, Laurie is highly marriageable and more and more obviously in love with Jo, who does not return his affection. Generations of readers have been tormented by Jo's seemingly inexplicable refusal to love Laurie. One can argue that Alcott sets up what looks like the perfect match between Jo and Laurie, then allows Jo to spurn his affections in order to explore the idea that a woman must marry a suitable man in order to be happy.

In New York, Jo finds a new kind of friend in Professor Bhaer. He is not only her friend but also her teacher. This student-teacher relationship mimics the relationship between Marmee and Mr. March, as well as the relationship between Jo and Mr. March. Surprisingly, in Bhaer's presence Jo becomes nearly conventional, conforming to a more accepted code of female behavior. She darns the professor's socks, for example, in order to show him her affection;

her willingness to engage in such a domestic and traditionally female chore reflects her newfound willingness to abide by nineteenth-century society's expectations of how a woman should act. Additionally, whereas earlier she takes on male roles in her plays, she now dresses as a female character, Miss Malaprop, at the New Year's Eve masquerade, revealing an ability and willingness to check her unconventional desires.

CHAPTERS 34–38

SUMMARY — CHAPTER 34: FRIEND
In New York, Jo begins to write sensationalist stories for a publication called the "Weekly Volcano." She is not proud of these stories, as they are not moral or profound in any way. They do, however, provide her with a lot of money. Later, she witnesses Mr. Bhaer defending religion in a philosophical conversation and is more impressed with him than ever. When he finds out that she writes sensationalist fiction, she is even more ashamed, and quits writing the tales. In June, she must return home. She tells Bhaer that she will see Laurie graduate, and Bhaer looks a bit jealous. He tells himself that he cannot hope to have Jo. She goes home feeling unsuccessful in writing, but very successful in having found such a good friend.

SUMMARY — CHAPTER 35: HEARTACHE
All of the Marches except Amy go to see Laurie graduate from college. He has done well there, having spent the last year working hard, probably to impress Jo. When he returns home, he finally confesses his love to Jo. She tries to stop him from speaking his mind, but he insists on telling her how he feels. She rejects his marriage proposals, telling him she doesn't love him in that way, which breaks his heart. He worries that she loves Professor Bhaer, and speaks scornfully of Bhaer's old age. Jo energetically defends the professor, but says she does not love him. After the rejection, Laurie mopes for a while until Mr. Laurence, to whom Jo has told of her conversation with Laurie, suggests that he and Laurie go to Europe for a while. Laurie reluctantly agrees and sadly leaves.

SUMMARY — CHAPTER 36: BETH'S SECRET
Coming home from New York, Jo has been surprised to find Beth even paler and thinner than before. She proposes to take Beth to

the mountains with the money that she has earned. Beth says that she does not want to go so far and asks to go to the seashore again instead. When they are on holiday, Beth confesses that she knows that she will die soon. Jo tells her that she will not, but Beth is certain that she will. Beth tells her that this realization was the reason she was melancholy the previous fall. She asks Jo to tell their parents so that she does not have to. But when they return home, Jo does not need to say anything. Their parents can see the change in Beth for themselves.

SUMMARY — CHAPTER 37: NEW IMPRESSIONS
Laurie meets up with Amy in Nice, in southern France, on Christmas. They each find that the other has changed quite a bit. Laurie notes that Amy has grown into a sophisticated and lovely young woman. Amy sees that Laurie is more somber, but she also starts to see him as a handsome gentleman instead of a childhood friend. He escorts her to a ball in her hotel that evening. She deliberately tries to look extremely pretty for him. At first, he is not as attentive as she wants him to be. Toward the end of the night, however, when she merrily and honestly confesses to the little tricks she employs to make herself pretty despite her poverty, he is touched, and fills up her dance card with his own name.

SUMMARY — CHAPTER 38: ON THE SHELF
Meg is spending so much time taking care of her babies that she rarely spends time with Mr. Brooke. After half a year of this behavior, he takes to going over to a friend's house at night. When he begins to spend less time with the children, Meg is saddened by his absence. Marmee figures out what the trouble is and suggests that Meg make an effort to be more interested in her husband's affairs and to be more presentable and loving. She says that Meg needs to work on her relationship with her husband as well as her relationship with her children. Meg resolves to try Marmee's advice: she puts the children to bed early, makes a nice dinner, and dresses up. John comes home and is pleased with what he sees. Demi, however, will not go to sleep. John takes over, reprimanding his son and making sure that he minds his mother. This night marks a change: Meg and John begin sharing the childrearing responsibilities and, as a result, spend more time together in their home.

ANALYSIS — CHAPTERS 34–38

In Chapter 34, Jo is still largely the same person as at the novel's beginning, pursuing her writing talent. The name of the magazine for which she writes—"Weekly Volcano"—suggests intense, even dangerous, creativity. Like a volcano, Jo possesses a wild and unpredictable temperament, and she is never really at ease. She is ready to erupt with her writing, and this magazine serves as the perfect outlet for her creativity.

In Chapter 35, in an extremely unusual literary event, Jo rejects Laurie's offer of marriage. Literary works are inevitably influenced by the values of the society in which their authors live, and at the time Alcott wrote, society did not look kindly on women who turned down eligible men. Women were expected to accept as their destiny the roles of wife and mother, and to dismiss any ideas of living an independent life that rejected these conventional roles. For this reason, very few female characters in literature from before the twentieth century display the sort of assertiveness and expression of individual desires that modern society, for the most part, values in women. It is therefore extremely significant that Jo rejects Laurie despite the fact that he is handsome, kind, loving, and rich, and that she rejects him for no other reason than that she does not love him as she wants to love a husband. Alcott depicts this decision as admirable. As Laurie says, everyone expects the marriage to happen—not only the characters in *Little Women,* but also everyone in the reading audience. Yet Alcott shows us that a strong woman is perfectly within her rights to flout the expectations of society.

In keeping with Alcott's progressive ideas about female roles in society, scholar Elizabeth Lennox Keyser has suggested that Beth's death results almost necessarily from the fact that the society in which she lives is evolving and thus rendering outdated the traditional values to which she clings outdated. Beth's quiet and old-fashioned character symbolically cannot survive in a world in which women begin to demand more from life than housework. She seems to have no place in the future and, by extension, no place in the second half of the novel.

Eager for her characters and her story not to be flat, Alcott attempts to show life's complexities by exploring both the positive and the negative aspects of certain experiences and attitudes. She realistically depicts marriage as a mixture of love, grumpiness, miscommunication, and gradual improvement. Similarly, she depicts Jo's separateness as a mixture of independence and loneliness. Earlier, Meg and John seem to be growing apart; now, however, they strike a balance in their relationship and begin to appreciate it again. Conversely, Jo, who earlier revels in her rebellious nature and defiance of social convention, now begins to envy Meg's family and see marriage in a more positive light. By putting her characters through this flux of emotion and attitude, Alcott makes her characters more realistic.

Alcott characterizes Meg and John's twins along traditional gender lines, which seems to reflect her understanding that progress toward a greater role for women would be achieved only gradually. Daisy is a stereotypical girl, while Demi is a stereotypical boy, who often tries to control his sister. While the family considers Demi's domination sweet, this behavior perpetuates the gender roles that Alcott has blurred with some success in the preceding generation, that of the March girls and Laurie.

CHAPTERS 39–47

SUMMARY — CHAPTER 39: LAZY LAURENCE
Although Laurie originally intends to spend a week in Nice, he ends up staying for a month in order to enjoy Amy's company. While he is there, Amy becomes more and more distressed at his laziness and bad humor. One day, they go for a drive to a scenic hilltop villa so that Amy can sketch. While there, Amy decides to lecture Laurie, telling him that he should be more attentive to his grandfather and that he should find a way to keep himself busy. Soon, she figures out that Jo has refused his marriage proposal, and she becomes somewhat more sympathetic. Still, she tells him not to waste his talents by sitting around moping. The next morning, she gets a note saying that he has heeded her advice and is on his way to see his grandfather. Although she will miss him, she is pleased that he has taken her advice.

SUMMARY — CHAPTER 40: THE VALLEY OF THE SHADOW
Because of Beth's failing health, the family sets up a lovely room for her. In it they place her piano, Amy's sketches, and other beautiful things. Meg also brings the babies over to brighten Beth's days. As time passes, Beth gets weaker, but she is not afraid of death. Jo writes a poem about all Beth has meant to her, which pleases Beth,

who worries that her life has been useless. Before Beth dies, she asks Jo to take care of their parents. Beth passes away peacefully.

SUMMARY — CHAPTER 41: LEARNING TO FORGET
Laurie is more active when he returns to Switzerland. He spends some time in Austria working on a requiem and an opera. He tries to make Jo his heroine, but she seems ill fit to be his artistic muse, or inspiration, so he begins to imagine a blonde damsel, although he does not name her. Laurie also begins to correspond with Amy frequently. When Fred Vaughn finally proposes, Amy turns him down because she does not want to marry for money. Amy and Laurie find out about Beth's death at nearly the same time, and Laurie goes to comfort Amy. They begin to spend much time together and fall in love. One day, Laurie and Amy are boating on a river. Laurie is doing the rowing, and Amy asks to help, telling him that he looks tired. They begin to row smoothly together, and Laurie asks Amy if she will always row in the same boat as him—that is, if she will marry him. Amy responds that she will.

SUMMARY — CHAPTER 42: ALL ALONE
Jo grows lonely at home, although she tries to make life easier for Marmee, Mr. March, and Hannah. One day, she confides to her father how much she misses Beth. Word arrives that Amy and Laurie are engaged, and Marmee is worried about how Jo will take the news. Jo is calm, though, and pleased that they are in love. She does wish that she could find a love of her own, but she does not begrudge Amy Laurie's affections. Jo begins to write more, and finds a style that is all her own. It has more truth in it than her previous sensationalist writing, and magazines publish many of her stories. She begins to think about Professor Bhaer sentimentally, hoping that he will come for her.

SUMMARY — CHAPTER 43: SURPRISES
Laurie comes into the house, surprising Jo. He tells her that he and Amy have married so that they could come home together without a chaperone. He tells Jo that she was right about her being unsuitable for him, and that he is happy to have Amy as his wife and Jo as his sister. With Amy, Laurie, and Mr. Laurence home, everyone celebrates all day and into the night. Mr. Laurence asks Jo to be his "girl" now that Beth is gone. As the family revels, Mr. Bhaer arrives unexpectedly. He says that he is in town on some business. Jo

warmly greets him. Everyone likes him very much. Jo notices that he is all dressed up as if he were courting. After a long evening, he asks if he may come back, as he is in town for a few days. Jo gladly tells him that he may.

SUMMARY — CHAPTER 44: MY LORD AND LADY

Amy and Laurie display their happiness at every moment, relishing each other's company. They discuss Mr. Bhaer, whom they think Jo will marry, and decide that they want to help the impoverished Bhaer financially. They also discuss the kind of philanthropy that they would like to practice, and conclude that they will support people who are ambitious and in need of money. In talking about all the good they will do, they feel closer than ever.

SUMMARY — CHAPTER 45: DAISY AND DEMI

Demi is interested in mechanics and philosophy, although he is only three. His grandfather adores him. Daisy adores Demi too, and allows herself to be dominated by him. She loves to help Hannah make food and keep house. Both children love to play with Jo, whom they call Aunt Dodo. She plays with them less when Bhaer is around, but they like him anyway, because he gives them chocolate drops. One day, Demi tells Jo and Bhaer that he has kissed a little girl. He asks Bhaer innocently whether big boys like big girls. Bhaer is a bit embarrassed but says that he thinks they do, an answer that delights Jo.

SUMMARY — CHAPTER 46: UNDER THE UMBRELLA

After much visiting, Bhaer stays away for three days. Jo heads out one day to run some errands, hoping to run into him. Just as rain begins to fall, she bumps into him, and he then covers her with his umbrella as they do some shopping together. He tells her that he has finished his business in town. He adds that has gotten a job teaching in the West, where he can make some money. She is distressed that he will go so far away, and begins to cry. Because she has displayed her feelings for him, Bhaer feels comfortable telling her that he loves her. She responds that she loves him too, and they decide to get married.

SUMMARY — CHAPTER 47: HARVEST TIME

> *Oh, my girls, however long you may live, I never can*
> *wish you a greater happiness than this!*
>   (See QUOTATIONS, p. 53)

Jo and Bhaer spend a year apart, pining for each other. Aunt March then dies unexpectedly, leaving her house, Plumfield, to Jo. Jo decides to turn it into a school for rich and poor boys alike. The family decides that it is a good idea. After several years, the school is up and running successfully. Mr. Laurence helps by paying some tuition for poor boys. In October, they have an apple-picking festival. The Marches, Brookes, Laurences, and Bhaers all arrive for a day of fun. They also all celebrate Marmee's sixtieth birthday. All of the sisters revel in their good fortune and count their blessings, congratulating Marmee on such a successful life. Jo says that she still hopes to write another novel but that she is very happy. Amy frets that her daughter, Beth, is ill, but plans to enjoy her for as long as she has her. Everyone expresses gratitude for the wonderful life they all share.

ANALYSIS — CHAPTERS 39–47

All of the characters who earlier wish for genius and success—Amy, Jo, and Laurie—now realize that they merely possess talent, not the genius for which they earlier hope. These realizations are the result of growing up and learning to accept small defeats. When old Mr. Laurence asks Jo to be his "girl" in place of Beth, Jo agrees, demonstrating that she has tempered some of her wildness with the gentle femininity she loved in Beth. Even Jo's writing style changes; she no longer writes tales of adventure and intrigue but, instead, writes in a simpler style that sounds similar to that of *Little Women* itself. Though one can argue that this change in writing style reflects a loss of independence for Jo, one can also argue that it demonstrates an ability to adapt her creativity to the world around her.

Alcott presents a new model of marriage with the pairing of Amy and Laurie. Amy serves as a mentor for Laurie, instead of the other way around. Scholar Elizabeth Lennox Keyser suggests that the two have the most egalitarian marriage of the novel, citing the fact that they row together as symbolic of their cooperation. Though this marriage holds promise, Alcott seems to layer it with a bit of regret suggesting that Laurie becomes his old playful self not in Amy's presence but only in Jo's.

In contrast to the stormy, childish encounter between Laurie and Jo when he proposes to her, Bhaer's proposal to Jo is touching and more grown-up. Jo goes out to seek Bhaer, demonstrating that she has some agency in the affair; when he proposes, the rain and mud prevent him from going down on his knee or giving her his hand, so they stand literally on an equal footing. Jo, furthermore, looks nothing like a romantic feminine heroine; she is bedraggled with rain and mud, but it makes no difference. This marriage, which begins with equality and primacy of the heart rather than primacy of appearances, is promising.

The fact that Jo inherits Aunt March's old house recalls the bond that exists throughout the novel between these two strong March women. What makes this detail most important is that property is customarily inherited by a man from another man. Aunt March's last act can therefore be seen as one of defiance against patriarchal norms. The endurance of this feminist stance is manifest in the fact that Jo too continues to defy gender conventions by sharing with her husband the typically male role of headmaster.

The end of the novel is both domestic and sentimental. Except for Beth, of course, all of the March girls have married, and two of them have had children. The girls' children hint at the eternal nature of such stories. Long after these characters have gone, others will take their place in the endless cycle of growing up, nesting, and raising one's children. As a sentimentalist novel, *Little Women* ends with everyone apparently getting what she deserves. Because of their continual efforts to be good, the March girls are rewarded with happy lives and loving families.

Important Quotations Explained

1. I'll try and be what he loves to call me, "a little
    woman," and not be rough and wild; but do my duty
    here instead of wanting to be somewhere else.

Jo speaks these words in Chapter 1 after hearing the letter from Mr. March, who is serving in the Civil War. Jo says that she would like to be doing something exciting, such as being in the Civil War like her father, instead of sitting at home. Jo points out that women cannot fight in the Civil War, and generally lead less adventurous lives than do men. In this statement, Jo also demonstrates a wish to make her father happy by acting stereotypically female. Jo struggles throughout the novel because she wants both to lead an adventurous, independent life and to help and please her family. In other words, the struggle for individual success conflicts with the duty and affection she feels for her family and with the domestic sphere that most women of the time accept.

Mr. March's letter comes immediately after all the March girls say that they want more out of life than what they have. After hearing his letter, they each decide to be content with what they have, demonstrating that the renunciation of their material dreams is learned, rather than natural, behavior.

QUOTATIONS

2.   I am angry nearly every day of my life.

Marmee makes this statement in Chapter 8 when she tells Jo that she too struggles with a quick temper. Throughout the novel, however, Marmee seems serene and composed, which suggests that the appearance of a docile woman may hide turmoil underneath. Marmee's admission makes Jo feel better, because she realizes that she is not the only one with a temper. At the same time, though, Marmee's words suggest that there is no hope for Jo—Marmee is still angry after forty years, and perhaps Jo will be too. Many feminist critics have noted this sentence as an expression of anger about nineteenth-century society's demand that women be domestic.

3. Money is a needful and precious thing,—and, when
    well used, a noble thing,—but I never want you to
    think it is the first or only prize to strive for. I'd rather
    see you poor men's wives, if you were happy, beloved,
    contented, than queens on thrones, without self-
    respect and peace.

Marmee speaks these words in Chapter 9, after Meg has returned
from a two-week stay at the Moffats' home. Marmee tells Meg that
she does not want any of her daughters to marry for material com-
forts, as was suggested by a guest at the Gardiners'. At a moment in
history when women's futures hinged solely on their choice of a husband, Marmee's statement is very compassionate and unusual.
After all, the other guests at the party easily assume that Meg must
be intending to marry for money.

Alcott does not completely sanction Marmee's statement. *Little
Women* depicts marrying poor as a serious burden for a nineteenth-
century woman to bear. One should not marry for money, but at the
same time, quarrels and stress come about from marrying a poor
man. Alcott does not depict romantic love without mentioning the
practical reality of living with little money. The daughter of an
improvident father, she knew firsthand the worry of having to
depend on someone else for a living.

QUOTATIONS

4. I'd have a stable full of Arabian steeds, rooms piled
    with books, and I'd write out of a magic inkstand, so
    that my works should be as famous as Laurie's music.
    I want to do something splendid before I go into my
    castle—something heroic, or wonderful—that won't
    be forgotten after I'm dead. I don't know what, but
    I'm on the watch for it, and mean to astonish you all,
    some day. I think I shall write books, and get rich
    and famous; that would suit me, so that is my
    favorite dream.

Jo speaks these words in Chapter 13 when the March girls and Laurie are discussing their dreams. In contrast to the typical dreams of
her sisters, Jo's dream is startlingly big and confidently expressed.
The horses Jo wants, and with which she is constantly compared,
represent the wild freedom for which she yearns. Significantly, Jo
does not mention a husband or children in her dream, but says she
wants books and ink. This powerful statement reaches well beyond
the confines of a woman's small living room and demands lasting
fame and independence in a man's world. Jo's sentences are very
direct and begin commandingly with the word "I."

   Jo also mentions the desire to have her work equal Laurie's. The
pursuit of an art is represented as an idyllic field in which men's and
women's work are considered equal. Also, Jo aligns going into a cas-
tle—getting married and having a house—with dying, for she wants
to do something great before either event happens to her.

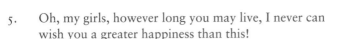

5.   Oh, my girls, however long you may live, I never can
      wish you a greater happiness than this!

These words from Marmee conclude the novel, at the end of Chapter 47, and also sum up the novel's message. Through the four
March sisters, Alcott presents many possible ways a woman can
walk through life. Both the novel and Marmee finally decide that
women must make some sacrifices for their families, in order to have
the happiest life possible. Perhaps Alcott sometimes wished her life
had turned out more traditionally and that she had married and had
children. This ending is ambiguous at best, however, since the novel
has called traditional values into question throughout.

KEY FACTS

FULL TITLE
Little Women

AUTHOR
Louisa May Alcott

TYPE OF WORK
Novel

GENRE
Sentimental novel; didactic novel; coming-of-age novel

LANGUAGE
English

TIME AND PLACE WRITTEN
1868–1869, Concord and Boston, Massachusetts

DATE OF FIRST PUBLICATION
1868–1869

PUBLISHER
Roberts Brothers

NARRATOR
Omniscient. The narrator knows everything and provides
analysis and commentary about the characters and their lives.

POINT OF VIEW
Third person. The narrator focuses on all the different
characters in turn.

TONE
Sympathetic and matter-of-fact; sometimes moralizing

TENSE
Past

SETTING (TIME)
During and after the Civil War, roughly 1861–1876

SETTING (PLACE)
A small New England town

PROTAGONIST
   Jo March

MAJOR CONFLICT
   The March sisters struggle to improve their various flaws as
   they grow into adults. Jo dreams of becoming a great writer and
   does not want to become a conventional adult woman.

RISING ACTION
   The sisters begin to mature; they meet Laurie, their next-door
   neighbor; Meg gets married.

CLIMAX
   Jo turns down Laurie's marriage proposal, confirming her
   independence.

FALLING ACTION
   Beth dies, and Amy marries Laurie; Jo marries Professor Bhaer;
   Jo founds a school for boys and puts her writing career on hold.

THEMES
   Women's struggle between familial duty and personal growth;
   the danger of gender stereotyping; the necessity of work; the
   importance of being genuine

MOTIFS
   Music, teaching, language

SYMBOLS
   Umbrellas, burning

FORESHADOWING
   When Laurie presents the March sisters with a postbox, the
   narrator hints that love letters will pass through the box in years
   to come. Laurie's promise to kiss Amy before she dies
   foreshadows their future marriage.

Study Questions & Essay Topics

Study Questions

1. Why does Alcott alternate between stories about each of the four March sisters throughout *Little Women*?

On the surface, the novel presents us with four different young girls so that every reader can identify with at least one of them and learn from their mistakes. In this way, *Little Women* resembles a didactic novel, a work meant to teach moral lessons. Besides showcasing different kinds of heroines, the four March sisters' stories each stand for the different options a woman had in the 1860s: she could stay at home, like Beth; she could marry, like Meg; she could become a modern and successful woman, like Amy; or she could struggle with her professional life and her personal life, like Jo.

Many readers claim Jo as their favorite, and it seems as though Alcott may have been doing more in *Little Women* than just introducing and developing four distinct possible female types. Jo is the only character whose personality most readers like more before she reforms and becomes more stereotypically feminine. With the character of Jo, Alcott creates a new sort of heroine, one who is flawed and human—and infinitely more lovable for those flaws.

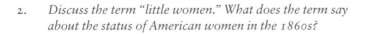

2. *Discuss the term "little women." What does the term say*
    about the status of American women in the 1860s?

A common term in the Victorian era, "little women" is used as a
term of endearment in the novel. Mr. March calls his daughters "little women" in the letter he sends them from the war. On the surface,
the term indicates the time between being a girl and being a woman,
a time that the novel portrays in the lives of the March sisters. However, "little" is also a diminutive word. It is interesting that Alcott
uses such a word when she seems interested in enlarging the status of
women in general. The novel is also crowded with references to
physical size: Jo, for example, is always described as large. She has
big feet, and her hands stretch out Meg's gloves. Additionally, Amy
tells Jo that there is "more of [her]" than there is of Amy.

But beyond her physical dimensions, Jo dreams big, and
throughout the story she is the sister with the most individual, creative promise. Conversely, Meg is a very conventional girl; likewise,
her shoes are described as too tight, and her house with John as too
cramped. Alcott mirrors Meg's limitations with the limitations of
her surroundings, suggesting that, in general, women are strictly
confined. Through the use of the term "little women," Alcott may
be suggesting that a woman's role is too small and confining for Jo,
as doubtless it was for many women of her day.

QUESTIONS & ESSAYS

3. *Discuss the role of the Civil War in* Little Women. *Who goes to the war, and who wants to? Why does Alcott deliberately put such a big war so far in the background of her story?*

The Civil War is never even mentioned by name in *Little Women*. At the beginning of the novel, all we know is that Mr. March is "far away, where the fighting [is]." At the beginning of the novel, Jo laments that she cannot participate in the action of the war; only men, such as Mr. March, can go. From that point on, we do not hear too much about the war except when Mr. March is sick. Instead, Alcott focuses heavily on domestic issues and personal matters in the lives of the March sisters. This situation is the opposite of that found in many men's novels of the time; in those novels, the war features prominently and matters of everyday life are de-emphasized. Since women were usually at home doing something mundane, their stories got lost in such male-dominated works. In *Little Women*, Alcott spotlights the women and the homefront; she puts the men aside in order to tell women's stories. In one striking example, Laurie is shown as the male outsider who longs to join the all-female March circle. This situation contrasts with the beginning of the novel, when Jo wants to join the men's circle of fighting. In her novel, Alcott documents women and their domestic lives, and shows that they are just as important and worthy of focus as men and their pursuits.

SUGGESTED ESSAY TOPICS

1. How does Jo represent the plight of the female artist in the 1860s? Does Amy represent the plight any differently? If so, how?

2. Discuss the similarities and differences between Jo and Amy. How do these differences lead to Laurie's love for Jo but eventual marriage to Amy?

3. Why does Jo marry Professor Bhaer instead of Laurie?

4. Discuss the character of Beth, the most conforming sister. Is her death at all symbolic?

5. Discuss the role of Mr. March. Why is he hardly present in the novel?

6. What are the elements, if any, of transcendentalist philosophy in *Little Women*?

7. Discuss the characters of Meg's twins, Daisy and Demi. How are the twins different from Jo and Laurie?

REVIEW & RESOURCES

QUIZ

1. What does Jo want to buy herself for Christmas?

    A. A horse
    B. A book
    C. Drawing pencils
    D. A new dress

2. Who presides over the Pickwick Club?

    A. Jo
    B. Marmee
    C. Laurie
    D. Meg

3. What does Beth bring over to Laurie when he is not feeling well?

    A. Flowers
    B. Mittens
    C. Kittens
    D. Slippers

4. What does Amy consider her greatest weakness?

    A. Her poverty
    B. Her nose
    C. Her dresses
    D. Her bad singing voice

5. What does Mr. Laurence give to Beth?

    A. Slippers
    B. His granddaughter's piano
    C. Voice lessons
    D. Books

6. Who proposes to Amy?

   A. Frank and Fred Vaughn
   B. Mr. Brooke and Laurie
   C. Fred Vaughn and Laurie
   D. Ned Moffat and Professor Bhaer

7. What is Jo's job in New York?

   A. Teaching and sewing
   B. Writing for a small newspaper
   C. Cooking and cleaning
   D. Bartending

8. What does Jo do with the prize money she wins for her first published story?

   A. She spends it in New York
   B. She sends Marmee and Beth to the beach
   C. She gives it to charity
   D. She gives it to Aunt March as repayment

9. How does Jo obtain the twenty-five dollars she gives to Marmee before Marmee goes to Washington, D.C.?

   A. She sells her hair
   B. She writes a story
   C. She baby-sits
   D. She sells baked goods

10. What do the Marches traditionally do before bedtime?

   A. Have a group hug
   B. Run a lap around the house
   C. Read a story aloud together
   D. Sing

11. What is Mr. Brooke's occupation?

   A. He is a college professor
   B. He writes domestic novels
   C. He is Laurie's tutor
   D. He does not have a job

12. Where is Jo and Mr. Bhaer's school located?

   A. Plumfield
   B. In the West
   C. In the Marches' house
   D. In Meg's house

13. How many people come to the party that Amy planned for her art class?

   A. One
   B. Two
   C. Three
   D. Four

14. When Beth seems moody, what does Jo think is causing the moodiness?

   A. That Beth thinks she is going to die
   B. That Beth is in love with Laurie
   C. That Beth's canary has died
   D. That Beth feels sorry for poor people

15. What does Amy do for which Jo swears she will never forgive her?

   A. She slaps Jo
   B. She trades limes at school
   C. She burns Jo's manuscript
   D. She burns Jo's hair

16. Who does Sallie Gardiner marry?

   A. Ned Moffat
   B. Laurie
   C. Fred Vaughn
   D. Frank Vaughn

17. What does Meg do for money before she is married?

   A. She works for Aunt March
   B. She works as a governess
   C. She sells her hair
   D. She sells limes

18. Why does Marmee take Amy out of school?

   A. She does not believe that children should be physically punished

   B. She thinks that the teacher should have left Amy's limes alone

   C. She thinks that the teacher provides bad mathematical instruction

   D. She thinks that Beth needs to teach someone

19. What is Jo's "one beauty," according to the novel?

   A. Her small feet

   B. Her aristocratic nose

   C. Her petite frame

   D. Her hair

20. What does Professor Bhaer always have in his pockets?

   A. His eyeglasses

   B. Flowers

   C. Chocolate drops

   D. A book

21. What type of music does Laurie try to write in Austria?

   A. A waltz and a hymn

   B. A requiem and an opera

   C. A concerto and a fugue

   D. A dance and a jig

22. From where is Professor Bhaer originally?

   A. Switzerland

   B. Austria

   C. Germany

   D. Italy

23. Who are the witnesses to Amy's will?

   A. Marmee and Mr. March

   B. Jo and Meg

   C. Laurie and Esther

   D. Aunt March and Aunt Carrol

24. With whom does Amy go to Europe?

    A. Florence and Aunt Carrol
    B. Laurie
    C. Jo
    D. Aunt March

25. Where in the March house does Jo do her writing?

    A. In Beth's room
    B. In the garden
    C. In the garret
    D. In her closet

SUGGESTIONS FOR FURTHER READING

BRODHEAD, RICHARD. *Cultures of Letters: Scenes of Reading and Writing in Nineteenth-Century America*. Chicago: University of Chicago Press, 1993.

DELAMAR, GLORIA T. *Louisa May Alcott and* LITTLE WOMEN: *Biography, Critique, Publications, Poems, Songs, and Contemporary Relevance*. Jefferson, North Carolina: McFarland, 1990.

ELBERT, SARAH. *A Hunger for Home: Louisa May Alcott and* LITTLE WOMEN. Philadelphia: Temple University Press, 1984.

KEYSER, ELIZABETH LENNOX. *Whispers in the Dark: The Fiction of Louisa May Alcott*. Knoxville: University of Tennessee Press, 1993.

SAXTON, MARTHA. *Louisa May*. Boston: Houghton Mifflin, 1977.

SHOWALTER, ELAINE. *Sister's Choice: Tradition and Change in American Women's Writing*. Oxford: Oxford University Press, 1994.

STERN, MADELEINE. *Louisa May Alcott*. Boston: Northeastern University Press, 1996.

———, ed. *Critical Essays on Louisa May Alcott*. Boston: G.K. Hall & Co., 1984.

STRICKLAND, CHARLES. *Victorian Domesticity: Families in the Life and Art of Louisa May Alcott*. University: University of Alabama Press, 1985.

SparkNotes Study Guides: